REAL ESTATE INVESTING MADE EASY
HOW TO GET RICH, FOR REAL

"Really educational and informative for both beginner and advanced real estate investors."

Brent Mondoux
CEO, N-VisionIT Interactive

Bruce M Firestone
B Eng (Civil), M Eng-Sci, PhD

Real Estate Investing Made Easy
How to get rich, for real

Dr Bruce M Firestone
B Eng (Civil), M. Eng-Sci, PhD

Booklet 1
How to Get Rich, For Real Series

Learn By Doing School Publications

Real Estate Investing Made Easy

A Learn By Doing School Book

Copyright © 2014 by Bruce M Firestone

All rights reserved, including the right to reproduce or transmit this book or portions thereof in any form whatsoever without written permission of the author and publisher.

For information, please contact:

Learn By Doing School Publications
Attention: Ms. Nina Brooks, ninabooks@rogers.com
Tel 1.613.566.3436 x 200
@ProfBruce
www.brucemfirestone.com

First Edition

Firestone, Bruce Murray, 1951—

Advance Reviews

"I think Real Estate Investing Made Easy is a well written guide on how to enter the real estate market for any first time investor. As a serial entrepreneur who operates in a field that covers both real property and the IT space, I think the analysis provided by Prof Bruce offers readers a great framework. When I finished my engineering degree, I followed the bungalow split-level model personally and it has worked out fantastically. My location is near a college and I've have had 100% occupancy rates for the last five years. My IRR is in the 40-50% p.a. range(it includes capital appreciation). I really enjoyed Firestone's humorous, clear and personal approach in presenting the material. That's hard to find," Jason van Gaal, founder, planus.ca.

"Prof Bruce's Real Estate Investing Made Easy—How to Get Rich, For Real is an excellent resource. With particular attention to thoroughgoing calculations contained within, Professor Firestone has taken a complex investing vehicle (real estate) and explained it in simple terms which makes it a must-read for both experienced and novice investors. It will help many, many people build an investment foundation for a better future for themselves and their families on a daily basis," Daniel Casal, B Com (Hon) Finance.

"This book is really educational and informative for both beginner and advanced real estate investors. It was a great read. I love the fact that Firestone shares all the details related to these real estate deals, including calculations used to prove the numbers. Really educational and informative," Brent Mondoux, N-VisionIT Interactive.

Dedication

I dedicate this booklet to all the people who are fed up with the stock market, mutual funds, tech bubbles, option trades, day trading, fund and financial advisors, t-bills, money market funds, savings account interest, bank fees, life insurance investments and pretty much every other type of investing save and except your own small or medium sized enterprise, one you own and control.

I have found you cannot save your way to wealth; you can only invest your way there. That is true for most people on this planet.

I did some research on wealthy families and found that many of them (in some countries as many as 61%) had substantially all of their wealth invested in real estate. It's the one asset class that does not run away from you when the going gets tough unlike, say, a typical consulting business where its prime assets go home every night. Real estate investing is the only thing I've ever done that made money for me and my family.

Having said this, in real estate, you make money when you buy not when you sell so there are some simple rules to follow—
1. buy when everyone else is selling;
2. sell when everyone else is buying;
3. buy what no one else is buying;
4. sell what no one else is selling;
5. buy before the bottom of the market;
6. sell before the top of the market;

If you follow these six rules, you are almost certainly going to successfully, "Buy low/sell high." This is easy to say, but hard to do since we all tend to move in herds—we want to do what everyone else is doing/wearing/listening to/going to. Resisting a herd mentality is really difficult.

People often ask me if I can help them get rich quick. They've read somewhere about some tech guy who sketched out a biz model on a napkin and flipped the startup for a few hundred million a year and a half later. Or they are watching those real estate pros on TV flipping barely renovated homes for unconscionable amounts of money in a few weeks. This is not realistic. At any one time there are probably 25 to 30 million smart Americans in their basements dreaming up the next big thing. And there are just as many smart Euros, Canucks, Chinese and Indians trying to do the same thing. I believe the odds of selling a startup for a few hundred million in less than two years is actually less than the odds of winning a major lottery like Powerball so if this is your "plan", buy a lottery ticket instead.

Oh, and as far as those real estate pros are concerned, many of them stack the deck in their favor—this is scripted "reality" television—reno costs are ridiculously low, transaction costs (like realtor fees, legal fees, land transfer taxes...) are ignored and prices are manipulated. Pollyanna would approve such a sunny approach to investing but your hard headed financial advisor will not. The only investments that are fun are the ones you make money with.

You can't *plan* on getting rich via a lottery win or by flipping real estate or tech assets or, for that matter, anything else. There is a rule about that. It goes like this, "Flippers, like gamblers, will flip til they flop." But if you are disciplined and work hard to build and hold a decent-sized real estate portfolio by following my simple recipe, you too get can rich, for real.

@ProfBruce
February 2014

Contents

Real Estate Investing Made Easy

Advance Reviews

Dedication

Introduction

Own Your Own Home

Buy Some Residential Rentals

Adding Additional Value to Your Principal Residence or Residential Rental Portfolio

Being Green

Adding In-Home Apartments or Granny Flats

Buy Some Commercial Property

Buy Some Land

Conclusion

Addendum 1

Addendum 2

About the Author

Real Estate Investing Made Easy

Introduction

If you were King or Queen of Exxon, what would you do with the unprecedented gusher of profits accruing to that company over the last two decades? In 2005, U.S. oil giant Exxon Mobil posted a quarterly profit of $9.9 billion, the largest in U.S. corporate history, on the back of record oil and gas prices. Profits were up 75% and revenues rose 32% to more than $100 billion.

So what would you have done with all this munificence? You might have decided to:

a. re-invest it in more oil exploration;
b. buy other oil companies;
c. increase dividends for shareholders;
d. buy stock back from existing shareholders;
e. raise wages and salaries for employees;
f. reduce prices for consumers;
g. hire more Washington lobbyists to ward off a windfall profits tax;
h. shop for the next Presidential candidate who would continue existing policies that resulted in unprecedented gains for the company; or
i. buy real estate.

I would guess that the CEO of Exxon was thinking about all of the above except for i. Now why should the King or Queen of Exxon even consider buying real estate?

Well, the real question I was asking myself was what would a person do if he or she wanted to create a lasting enterprise—one that would be around for several centuries or millennia?

This is a non trivial problem. Think how few corporations make age 50 let alone 100, 200 or more. Actually, think of how many make the age of 5.

But before tuning our minds to the idea of making Exxon a longterm play; let's just put in perspective what $10 billion in PROFITS each quarter means. There are 52 weeks per year or 13 weeks per quarter on average so Exxon made about $770,000,000 in profit each *week*. This is like having someone coming to your home 77 times a week, ringing the doorbell each time before giving you a check for $10 million in lottery winnings. Every two hours and 18 minutes, 24/7 a courier is there with your money. Within a week or two, you would be pleading with them to stop coming; it would drive you crazy. Even baseball players don't make that much.

So if you wanted to create a sustainable enterprise, say one that would last as long as the Holy Roman Catholic Church (a couple of millennia or so), what would you do?

For readers of the popular business press who are older than 35, you will have realized by now that firms that reporters were raving about a few quarters or at most a few years ago are now treated like neighborhood lepers. Remember the celebrity CEO? He is in jail.

Companies have a birth, life and a death. They are subject to cycles. Great names like DEC, Arthur Anderson, Systemhouse, TWA, Pan Am, Enron, Sperry and Burroughs can disappear (to be replaced sometimes with poorly chosen names like Unisys).

What do the House of Windsor, Emperor of Japan, Hudson's Bay Company*, Canadian Pacific and the Holy Roman Catholic Church have in common other than they are all extraordinarily long lived institutions? They all have significant ownership interests in real estate.

(* The oldest company in North America and one of the oldest anywhere is the Hudson's Bay Company, which was incorporated on May 2nd, 1670. A Royal Charter from King Charles II granted the company a monopoly over the fur trade in the region where all rivers and streams flow into Hudson's Bay, an area of 3.9 million km². The Company has significant real estate interests.)

People, markets, weather, sun spots are all subject to cycles. Real estate is subject to cycles too. But one thing about real estate—it generally doesn't go out of fashion. Since villages, towns and cities began to form about 10,000 years ago, real estate has generally tended to increase in value if we exclude factors that led to abrupt collapse and depopulation due to war, famine, disease, pestilence or natural disaster.

I think there is something fundamentally different about real estate; something that separates it from every other type of investment that humans might think to make. Here are a few things for the CEO of Exxon to consider if he or she wanted to make Exxon a long lived real estate vehicle:

1. Ownership of real estate could become the chosen investment vehicle for their windfall profits.

2. There would be little trading in real estate—it would be a long term hold thereby minimizing capital gains taxation.

3. Properties would be rented or leased including the leasing (but not sale) of land (the Catholic Church has entered into long term land leases for generations).

4. Investment would be in jurisdictions where there is respect for the rule of law, contracts, property and human rights.

5. Significant investment would be in the residential sector—it is less volatile than commercial real estate—people always need a home. You've probably heard that while people are prepared to work in cave they want to live in a castle.

6. Investment would favor high growth, desirable cities over low growth, less attractive ones.

7. Careful consideration would be given to income tax and realty tax considerations. Once the Queen of England gave up her right to be income tax exempt in a colossal error in judgment, she unknowingly destroyed the family's future guarantee of wealth.

8. There would be no (or very little leveraging of assets), no negative pledging or any other form of debt registered against the properties.

9. Properties would be self insured against loss. Insurance is a way for large companies to appropriate part of the value of your property each year without compensating you. If you are the U.S. Government, for example, you self insure. Large companies could do the same.

10. Property management is a core competency and would never be contracted out.

11. Investment would be in a maximum of two or three dozen cities in a small number of countries—enough to give geographic and political diversity but not so many as to be unmanageable.

12. Management would be highly centralized, conservative and experienced in real estate. The portfolio would consist of existing income property, property to be developed (both greenfield and brownfield sites) and land with the bulk of the assets held in the income category.

Those are a dozen rules that can apply to any large investor in real estate. For smaller investors, they would inevitably change this set of rules. For example, real estate is an intensely local business so it would make no sense for them to be in more than one or at the most two or three markets.

Also, small players (who want to get bigger) must by necessity use leverage to increase their ROE, Return on Equity. They are almost certainly better off with five properties with 20% equity in each than one property paid for via 100% equity. This assumes that they are not upside down on equity (i.e., that their cost of borrowing is greater than their ROE) so leverage represents a positive gearing for their investments. So if you were going to create a new state called Exxon Nation, you could do worse than follow the 12 rules above.

I met with a couple in their early 40s and they asked me to lay out a program for them so that in addition to building their portfolio of financial assets, they could add a real estate mix to it as well. They agreed that the latter would *not* include a "flip this house/as-seen-on-TV" approach—they would take a longer view.

I told them that simple real estate investing is based on four principal elements:

1. Buy a home (townhome or condo) as your principal residence and pay off your mortgage.
2. Buy some residential rental property with 5% to 25% down.
3. Buy some commercial rental property with 25% to 35% down.
4. Buy some land with 50% down.

The purpose of this booklet is to help you craft your own real estate strategy, to understand the fundamentals of successful real estate investing and then give you some guidelines on how to implement your program and achieve your goals.

Own Your Own Home

They already own their own home so this is a good start. Next, I want them to pay off their mortgage because this will create for them 'unearned rent' which is also tax free.

Unearned rent* is a British term and is a bit difficult to understand but, nevertheless, very real. Let's say you own a $300,000 principal residence and you think: 'Ah ha, if we move out and rent it, we'll earn extra income.' This is a bad idea.

Say, you do move out and rent it for $2,000 per mth. Your income goes up by $24,000 per year but if you are in a 40% tax bracket, you only net $14,400 (I am simplifying calculations here) but wait! You have to live somewhere. So you go out and rent something just as nice as the principal home you just leased out which, lo and behold, costs you $2,000 per month (in non tax deductible) rent. So you are paying $24,000 per year in after tax rent and receiving just $14,400 in rent (also after tax) which means you are $9,600 *worse off* than if you had just stayed in your original home. This is the 'rent' that you collect from yourself (aka, unearned rent) by just staying in your own home in the first place!

I realize that it looks kind of fishy but it is very real. You are, in fact, collecting an extra $9,600 in untaxed income* *every year* you live in your own home once your mortgage is paid off. Don't believe me? I have many clients in their 40s, 50s, 60s, 70s and older who, after paying off their mortgages (lucky them), suddenly 'feel' richer. I explain that they really are.

(* Governments in Australia, the UK and Switzerland have at one time or another thought about taxing this unearned rent but civil unrest has prevented them from doing it so far or, where they actually did it, to repeal the laws soon after. Calculations are more complex in the U.S. where mortgage interest is tax deductible but here is another real estate (or any other type of) investing tip—never do anything to lose money because you might get a tax advantage. Making a profit is a good thing and paying taxes means you've been successful. Still having said this (as my dad once told me), "Be proud to pay your taxes, son, just don't pay any more than you have to.")

Now I ask my students, "How many of you can save $775 a month?" Few hands go up. But when I ask, "How many of you can pay rent of $775 per month?" many hands (most of them) go up. So the problem with saving is first, most people are bad at it and second, even if they did manage to save $775 a month for say three years, it might not matter anyway.

Here's a simple spreadsheet on this. In this scenario, Sally Supersaver saves $775 per month for three years. She puts her funds in what her bank calls her "Power Savings Account" that yields a princely 0.7% p.a. in interest. Ignoring bank fees and simplifying interest calculations, Sally has put away a respectable $27,900 in principal over the term of her plan on which she has netted $392.43 in interest so she has $28,095.76 in her savings account at the end of three years. This is probably more than enough for a nice downpayment on her first home in most cities in the U.S. and Canada.

Year	Monthly Savings	Months per Year	Total Saved	Cumulative Savings	Interest	Interest Rate
1	$775	12	$9,300	$9,365.10	$65.10	0.70%
2	$775	12	$9,300	$18,665.10	$130.66	0.70%
3	$775	12	$9,300	$28,095.76	$196.67	0.70%
Total			$27,900	$28,095.76	$392.43	

The problem is that Sally has her eye on some type of overhyped new Apple product, a nice holiday in the DR (Dominican Republic) and she would like to buy a new car to replace the old beater she's had since her college days. In all likelihood, when we check back on Ms Supersaver in a couple of years and most of her savings are GONE.

So a big element of buying a home/condo/townhome/co-op apartment is *forced* savings—every month you pay your mortgage, some of that money goes to retire your principal and that belongs to you not the bank. But wait, there's more. If residential real estate increases in value in your city, that increase in value also belongs to you not the bank.

So let's see what happened to Ms Holly Homeowner in the same five year period. She uses her savings ($27,830) to buy a starter home for $220,000. She puts 10% down and uses the rest to pay for legal fees, transfer taxes and any surprises that come her way during this exciting time in her life. Instead of paying rent to a landlord, she pays it to herself—this is an opportunity cost, i.e., what she would have had to do with the money if she had not bought her first home since she has to live somewhere and being a homeless person is not an option.

In five years, she will have paid off $19,766 of principal on her mortgage of $198,000 and because Holly is a smart buyer (having chosen a solid structure in a good neighborhood), real estate inflation has increased the value of her property by 3.5% per year. In real estate, *you make money when you buy not when you sell* so buying wisely is very important. If you overpay in real estate, you will *never* catch up, never.

On the 5th anniversary of purchase, Holly sells her place for $261,000. After paying her realtor 5% and her attorney $783 for his work on her escrow closing, she nets $247,000. Oh yes, almost forgot, she also has to pay back the bank (darn). She now owes them $198,000 less the principal she repaid during the 5 years she owned her place or about $178,000. So it looks like she will net around $70,500.

But Holly is a disciplined person—she's been paying rent to herself of $775 a month for the whole 5 years so she's been making a cash-on-cash return in her homeowner account of about $1,250 per year so her total cash on hand on the day of closing shows up as $75,443.33 in Quick Books. (Holly is also smart about keeping good records.)

So while Sally Supersaver did well for three years before losing it all over the next two years on a spending splurge, Holly Homeowner has turned her $27,830 into $75,443.33 during the same period. Now I'm telling you, it's hard to save 75,000 bucks and even harder to resist the urge to blow it.

Here are the calculations—

Ms Holly Homeowner

First Time Homebuyer	$	220,000.00				
Equity		($22,000.00)	10.00%			
Legal Fees		($880.00)	0.40%			
Transfer Taxes		($2,200.00)	1.00%			
Misc		($2,750.00)	1.25%			
Total Equity		($27,830.00)				
Mortgage	$	198,000.00	2.25%		35	yrs
Mortgage Payment		($8,053.09)	per year			
Real Estate Inflation		3.50%				
Realtor Fees		5%				
Selling Price	$	261,290.99	after		5	yrs
Realtor Fees		($13,064.55)				
Legal Fees		($783.87)	0.30%			
Net Proceeds	$	247,442.56				
PPMT						
1		($3,779.31)				
2		($3,864.34)				
3		($3,951.29)				
4		($4,040.19)				
5		($4,131.10)				
Total Principal Repaid		($19,766.23)				
Principal Owed	$	178,233.77				
Rental Rate		$775	per month	(opportunity cost)		
		$9,300	per year			

There are three types of returns in real estate—

1. cash-on-cash returns,
2. real estate inflation,
3. forced savings.

In the above example, Holly is making $1,246.91 a year net on her home. She invested a total of -$27,830 (the negative sign just means it's an outflow of funds) so her cash-on-cash return is about 4.5% p.a. Cash-on-cash (sometimes called an ROE, Return on Equity) is a measure of how much money you are generating out of your investment, money that you can touch, feel and *spend*.

Now her house has gone up in value over the five years she has owned it by $41,290.99 (see below). An observant reader will find me (I'm easy to find on the Internet) and then message me that I show that Holly's house has gone up in value more than what she actually realizes in a sale. Correct. This is the Warren Buffet School of investing—a buy and hold approach. If you do that you won't be paying out any transaction costs (legal or realtor fees) and you won't be paying any (capital gains or income) taxes either so you actually make more money by not selling. More on this later. Suffice it to say at this point, Holly is seeing real estate inflation returning an average of almost 30% per year. Wow.

Cash-on-Cash Return	$1,246.91			
Equity	($27,830.00)			
Cash-on-Cash Return	**4.48%**	**p.a.**		
Real Estate Inflation	$ 41,290.99		5	yrs
Real Estate Inflation	$ 8,258.20	per year		average
Equity	($27,830.00)			
Real Estate Inflation	**29.67%**	**p.a.**		
Forced Savings	$19,766.23		5	yrs
Forced Savings	$3,953.25	per year		average
Equity	($27,830.00)			
Forced Savings	**14.20%**	**p.a.**		
IRR				
0	($27,830.00)			
1	$1,246.91			
2	$1,246.91			
3	$1,246.91			
4	$1,246.91			
5	$70,455.70	$75,443.33		
IRR				
	23.2%	**p.a.**		

Lastly, Ms Homeowner is being "forced" to save $19,766.23 over five years (as she pays off her mortgage) which nets her another 14.2% p.a.

Now these three types of returns are not strictly additive. You can't say that Holly is getting 4.48% + 29.67% + 14.20% p.a. in part because the middle number only happens if she *doesn't* sell and partly because her real return is a kind of weighted average of the three.

The best way we have found to measure rates of return in all types of investing is probably the IRR, Internal Rate of Return. The IRR is the discount rate that makes all future cashflows exactly equal to the initial investment. The higher you need to discount future cashflows to make them exactly equal initial investment, the better your project is (from a financial perspective).

So Holly's IRR is found by solving this equation:

$-\$27,830.00 + \$1,246.91/(1 + irr)^1 + \$1,246.91/(1 + irr)^2 + \$1,246.91/(1 + irr)^3 + \$1,246.91/(1 + irr)^4 + \$70,455.70/(1 + irr)^5 = 0$

This is solved by iteration which is another way of saying guessing. Happily, you don't actually have to solve it manually. Any spreadsheet program will do it for you. Computers guess too—they solve it by iteration but they do it a lot faster than you or me.

Holly's IRR is 23.2% p.a. which is a lot more than what Sally gets on her Power Savings Account (0.7%) which is just another way of saying, "*Most people can't save their way to wealth, they have to invest their way there.*"

Now these calculations are simplified—they ignore tax implications and other costs. Tax treatment varies from nation to nation—some countries like the U.S. allow mortgage interest to be deducted from taxes owing, others like Canada do not but they also don't levy capital gains taxes on the sale of principal residences.

Homeowners also have other costs they have to worry about like maintenance and repairs, property taxes, insurance and utilities. But more landlords these days are charging tenants for some (or all) of these costs in addition to basic rent and every tenant should have tenant's insurance if not to cover their own stuff to insure and protect themselves against claims for damage to the building, other tenants' property or in case someone injures herself or himself while visiting.

But the basic facts are there—discipline, real estate inflation and forced savings can produce big changes in your personal financial wellbeing. If Holly ever needed to get access to cash fast, she can do it using a HELOC (Home Equity Line of Credit) or remortgage her place and take out some cash. As the equity in her home increases, she can borrow against it.

There are appraisers who do "driveby appraisals" and will give a homeowner a written appraisal of FMV (Fair Market Value) in 24 to 48 hours (they charge more for this kind of superfast service) and there are lenders who can approve HELOCs very quickly. This type of thing is usually only necessary in a family emergency*—I've seen people in trouble get money this way in 72 hours. Hopefully, Holly won't face this but if she does, she will take comfort from the fact that she knows it's there.

(* Unfortunately, people with gambling problems or drug ones often end up owing money to, shall we say, non-traditional lenders. When the choice is paying up or having your legs broken, accessing their home equity is the route they go. Most people in this situation are not going to see their HELOCs or mortgage approvals based on the FMV of their homes. Instead, lenders will use QSV, Quick Sale Value.

Most traditional lenders look at mortgage approvals based on three things—your creditworthiness (your Beacon or Credit Score), your other monthly obligations, your income. There are other lenders (called asset lenders) who will look at the FMV of the underlying asset and the LTV (Loan to Value) ratio. They will place less emphasis on or have no regard for your personal credit rating, income and other obligations. LTV ratios today are anywhere from 65% (on commercial property) to 75% on owner-occupied residential property. First time homebuyers may see LTVs of 90 or even 95%. Asset based lenders will usually go as high as 85% thinking that even if the real estate market corrects by 10%, they can always foreclose, sell the property and get out whole.)

Now in my view there are two kinds of debt—good debt and debt that leads to problems. Good debt is the type of debt that Holly has—a mortgage secured against an asset so that if bad things happen to her or her family, she can sell and (hopefully) the debt goes away.

Bad debt is money owed on things like credit cards which are personally secured by you so in the event that you lose your job, too bad, you are still on the hook for it. By the way, even if you declare personal bankruptcy (generally a very bad idea), you may have to pay some of your credit card and other unsecured debt anyway. Bankruptcy trustees and judges will understand that you are in trouble but they may expect (insist) you put some of your *future* earnings away to pay off your creditors so this is the type of debt to avoid in almost all cases.

In the U.S., mortgage debt is non-recourse debt which means that even if the sale proceeds are not enough to retire the mortgage balance, the lender can not come after Holly if she were to default on her mortgage. It's another reason to say mortgage debt is good debt. However, this is not true in other nations like Canada where Holly would be responsible for any deficiency *personally*. So there are caveats that come with the statement that mortgage debt is good debt.

Still the number one source for equity (worldwide) for startups, for business owners and for entrepreneurs is home equity so if Holly decides to start a business, buy a business or buy some investment property and she accesses her equity via a HELOC or by remortgaging for a higher principal amount, this is good debt. Even in nation's where mortgage interest is not tax deductible from income, interest paid on money accessed this way (where the intent is to invest for profit) becomes tax deductible so it is possible to turn your mortgage interest into a tax deduction afterall.

Any money that is withdrawn this way comes out tax free so even if capital gains taxes are levied on your principal residence upon its sale, you don't have to sell the asset to access your money. You can pull it out tax free instead. This is an old Warren Buffet trick (he's been doing this with Berkshire Hathaway since the 1950s with incredible results). So it's yet another reason to "build and hold". I also put it this way, "Flippers, like gamblers, will flip til they flop."

When you see those shows on TV where they buy, renovate and flip houses for short term gain, you are seeing a fiction. They vastly underestimate reno costs and transaction costs (like finance fees, legal fees and realtor costs) as well as the time it takes to do those improvements. They often overstate sale prices and rents too. So the right approach is to build and hold and, believe me, you will get rich, slow.

Buy Some Residential Rentals

I am not actually as keen on residential rentals. Cap rates are often bad, rent control* in many U.S. cities like they have in New York City makes it harder to get rid of horrible tenants or raise rents and you generally have to re-lease the place and make it move-in ready once per year which costs you money in terms of maintenance and lost rent due to vacancy. But it forms part of your portfolio because, if I didn't include it, my clients and students would do it anyway and just not tell me so I might as well give them a few pointers so they can avoid the worst pitfalls.

(* Some big landlords have come to love rent control. One of them I know, someone who has more than 36,000 rental units, said it was the single *best* thing that ever happened to his company. It created an artificial scarcity of rental product, drove competitors out of the business allowing him to buy them out at a fraction of the cost of building new apartments, reduced vacancy rates, allowed him to pass on "government-approved" rent increases (padded by flow through costs for maintenance and repairs as well as improvements to the units) which most tenants meekly accepted. He now has free cashflow from his portfolio north of $40 million per *month*, that's real spending money.)

So here are some suggestions:

a) Get a property manager who carefully vets tenants for you or, if you are your own property manager, make sure you are thorough. You are far better off to leave a unit vacant than to rent to a bad tenant. If you do have a poor tenant, an experienced property manger will know how to navigate the rent control process to evict them. Knowing what is and isn't allowed is an important part of being successful when you appear before your local rental tribunal on an eviction matter. An attorney can also advise you in this regard. You should start proceedings against a tenant who misbehaves, disrupts quiet enjoyment of the premises by other tenants or for non-payment within days, a week at most.

b) Don't ever buy a property that doesn't cashflow. The idea that you can make up for monthly cashflow deficiencies by capital appreciation is flawed. It will crater your IRR, Internal rate of Return.

c) Buy low/sell high. As I said above, you make money in real estate when you buy not when you sell. So if you get into a competitive bidding war and get carried away and pay too much for that cool triplex or duplex, you're sunk.

d) Try to use all the leverage you can—financial institutions in North America will still lend to people with good credit (i.e., good Beacon) scores with just 5%, 10% or 15% down. So rather than buy one res rental unit with 25% down, buy five of them with 5% down if you can.

e) If you own five units and one becomes vacant, your vacancy rate has jumped from 0 to 20% but if you only own one unit and it becomes vacant, your vacancy rate has leaped from 0 to 100% which is bad.

f) By using lots of leverage, you actually will have more cashflow and more forced savings and more wealth effect provided you live in a stable economic environment (like, say, Boston, San Francisco or Portland not Arizona or Nevada) and provided you followed my earlier rule—buy low.

g) You or your property manager should visit each of your rentals, once per month. Tell your tenants in advance (some jurisdictions require you do this in writing) that you will be visiting once per month to collect rent personally, to inspect the unit every time you visit and to fix any problems immediately. Don't be lazy, do it. If prospective tenants don't want this, no problem. They can rent somewhere else. Friends of mine owned a 5-bedroom home near a college that they rented out to students for $500 per room per month. They visited every month bringing dinner with them (kids are always hungry). They developed nice relationships with them, monitored the condition of the place, never lost a single month's room rent and even helped them with homework and personal problems when warranted.

h) When I owned a rental property in a tough neighborhood, I co-opted the locals including teens by hosting a FREE BBQ and blocko (short for block party) every summer. I gave all the kids (some of whom were gang members no doubt) free burgers and flying discs and told them if they needed anything to let me know. In the years I owned the place, I had zero graffiti and vandalism—local guys looked out for it for sure. The few hundred bucks it cost was way less expensive than higher insurance premiums. (Note: you can often get a permit to close a street for a blocko from your local municipality. They're usually free. You can invite everyone in the area by the simple expedient of a flyer drop (in some neighborhoods like the one we were in, websites/mobile apps/email/facebook/twitter/linkedin/online invitations won't gonna work). Free food and beverage with some music and games (we liked Ultimate played on the street and Paddle Tennis) will bring people out. But don't serve any alcohol—this leads to fights and opens you up to huge liability.)

i) If you build or buy a duplex/triplex/multiplex, make sure you sound, smell and fire separate your units and they comply with building code and health code as well as fire and safety code. If you are purchasing an existing building, make sure you have a building inspector that knows these codes and can provide you with advice and costs estimates to make your units legal. If you discover any surprises, it's best to find these out during your conditional period when you can either abandon the deal or ask for a price abatement (reduction) from the Seller. Fire separation is improved by adding an extra layer of drywall. If you add it so that sheet boundaries do *not* line up, you will improve not only fire protection, you will limit sound transmission and smells between units. There are lots of simple, inexpensive things that you can do that not only improve safety for your tenants; they make their lives more enjoyable. By not venting one unit into another one, for example, automatically reduces sound, smell and fire issues…

j) With residential rentals, you see a return when: 1. monthly cashflow (aka cash-on-cash return) from rental and other income (like parking and laundry revenues) exceed expenses, 2. your tenants pay their rent on time so you can pay your mortgage down (forced savings) and 3. when your real estate appreciates (which is a wealth effect). Almost no one can save their way to wealth but many have invested their way there. You can read my fictional story about an imaginary world called Grassel made up of Grasshoppers, Squirrels and Ants plus Mensa Ants: http://www.eqjournal.org/?p=2760 which graphically demonstrates on how this and clearly explains why the "1%" are so wealthy.

My friends who owned the split-level home near the college made about $400 per month in free cashflow during the three years they owned their place. The students all accepted 12 month leases even if they were from out of town so they would be sure to have place to live when they came back each fall.

Their mortgage paydown was $18,000 during that period (remember, it's really the students paying off their mortgage for them) and they made a capital gain (the wealth effect) of about $38,000 on the sale after all expenses were paid (e.g., legal and realtor fees on completion of the transaction).

They originally financed 85% of the purchase price, so the cash they put down was around $40k of their own money. Thus over three years, they made $14,400 from their monthly free cashflow (cash on cash), $18,000 from paydown of their mortgage and $38,000 from capital appreciation. This represents a tidy $70,400 (before tax) profit/gain in three years on an initial investment of $40,000. Try to match that by investing the same $40,000 in the stock market (at the same level of risk) or by buying t-Bills which pay 0.5% to 2.5% p.a. There's just no comparison.

But what's also interesting is that they don't have $70,400 at the end of three years—they have $70,400 (assuming they did not spend their free monthly cashflow) plus their original equity of $40,000. So they actually have $110,400 of cash in hand (less whatever taxes they owe on the money they made– part of which are incomes taxes and part of which are presumably less onerous capital gains taxes.)

Now let's assume through some kind of modern miracle, my friends managed to *save* the same amount during those three years that they made by investing in their rental property. They woulda have saved it by deferring gratification except here's the thing—people don't *like* deferring gratification so they would probably have *spent* their money. If you read my Grassel story, you'll see that the Mensa Ants, who are really good investors, own just about everything while savers have much less and Grasshoppers (who spend everything they make) have nothing.

Adding Additional Value to Your Principal Residence or Residential Rental Portfolio

It doesn't matter what kind of business you are in, you need to add some differentiated value—something that makes you standout from the crowd. In terms of your principal residence or your residential rental portfolio, I have a list of a dozen things I consider for every project. I ask, can I add—

1. basement apartment with separate entrance,
2. landscaped paving stone area suitable for parking in the front yard, side or rear yards,
3. bench seat with storage beneath,
4. foundation stone,
5. blinds,
6. hardwood floors,
7. awning,
8. balcony,
9. deck,
10. barbeque,
11. bike rack,
12. "lipstick" to otherwise improve curb appeal?

I also ask, can I:

1. Stage the home?
2. De-clutter it?
3. Patch and paint it?
4. Clean it?
5. Improve the yard by weeding the garden and cutting the lawn?

If you want to be successful in real estate, you need a good team around you, one you can trust and who are really good at what they do. Your team should include: a deal-making attorney, a residential realtor who knows what s/he is doing, a commercial realtor (same thing), a mortgage broker who gets deals done, a creative designer, a talented group of contractors, a competent property manager (if you are not doing this yourself), a home stager and a landscaper who will help you not only maintain the outdoor space but improve it. You will also need good relationships with suppliers for building materials and appliances as well as with your city's buildings and plans departments so when you need something from them (like a building permit, a license or an inspection), you get it on a timely basis.

Practically the worst thing you can do with your own home or your rental portfolio from a financial point of view is over-improve it. Swimming pools are costly to install, heat, maintain and almost always represent a negative return on investment. There are many types of home improvements that contribute 50% or less of their cost to value and some like pools can actually be a net negative. Pools are also seen as a danger to children, your own and neighbors' so to many potential buyers, when they see a pool, they see a money pit and a monster.

When clients of mine are getting ready to sell, they'll ask me, "Do you think I should redo the kitchens and bathrooms?" Unequivocally, the answer is, "No." If you rip out your kitchen counter tops and put in $8,000 of green granite instead, watch when a potential buyer comes in and says, "I love this place except I hate green!" You've just wasted 8 grand.

So look at my lists and do (low cost) minimalist things like de-clutter, patch and paint, cut the lawn, weed the garden, clean up the place and stage it. That's about it.

The reason I have things like adding a foundation stone or a bench seat with storage underneath is that I think every real estate investor/owner/manager should have her or his own signature—things like this are not expensive to add but somehow they make a tenant or new owner feel like it is "home", that it is a place to care about. It's part of building a brand and brands matter—they create trust and trust creates an opportunity to make a sale…

If you could achieve the brand power of Apple, you too can charge more than the competition for the same thing, a lot more. So curb appeal and the warmth of interior spaces matter a lot in this business. If a prospective tenant or buyer comes to view one of your properties and the public room is littered with garbage, a window is broken and covered by plastic, the front door is hanging on one hinge and the place smells like cats live there instead of people, what kind of deal are you going to be able to do and do you really want to do rent to people who don't mind things like that?

Sometimes, you can up your returns just by naming things. When clients of mine recently bought a five-plex, they bought the place from an elder who had owned it for almost 70 years. They asked his permission which he gave and now there's a sign out front which reads Henderson House* in a lovely script. This together wih a lipstick renovation have increased rents by nearly a factor of two over the last four years. People don't live at 243 Springfield Road*, they live at Henderson House.

(* Names have been changed for privacy reasons.)

In Lord of the Rings, JRR Tolkien had the elves running around Middle Earth naming everything. They thought it was important. The elves (and Tolkien) were right. When you name something, you give it a life of its own.

Naming a project, a building, a subdivision, a new company, a new product, a new organization, a road, a new service, a baby, is important. Think, "Netflix" and maybe you recall good feelings about choice/budget/no adverts. Think, "Qwikster" and you might think avarice, rip off and lousy PR. Netlfix CEO Reed Hastings announced less than a month after deciding to split Netflix into two separate companies (Netflix and Qwikster), the latter was dead.

A lot of thought can and should go into names, slogans, tag lines and so forth. When I ran a mini storage company called Blue Heron Storage Corp, its tag line was *"Outta Site"* which had three meanings—off site, out of sight and (in 1960s language) far-out.

Being Green

I also get asked about greening your portfolio. I have to say that almost everyone who talks about green building is really dealing in greenwashing. There are almost no builders who do anything other than talk about being green. Perhaps they add a bit more insulation in the walls and attic and call it a day.

In the commercial real estate sector, it's worse if that is even possible, since landlords who have triple net leases actually have an incentive not to be green. They charge an administration fee on operating costs and utilities so the higher heating, air conditioning, maintenance and repair costs are, the more money they make. So turn up your t-stat in winter, turn it down in summer; it's good business for your landlord.

In a low rise residential setting, some things you might consider that can actually work in terms of lowering your environmental footprint include—

1. all-off button (one switch in a convenient location so that when you are leaving a building, you hit that one switch and everything (except essential services) are turned off),
2. getting rid of grass (and hence grass cutting, fertilizing, watering, weeding) substituting local flora (this is called a xeriscape) or hard surfaces,
3. capturing rainwater and using it for irrigation (if you need it),
4. low flush toilets with two flow settings,
5. solar hot water,
6. solar panels,
7. solar air wall,
8. additional insulation,
9. heat recovery unit,
10. heat pump,
11. water-saving faucets,
12. LED lighting,
13. intermittent spin washer,
14. low energy-consumption appliances,
15. install motion sensors to turn off lights,
16. get a programmable t-stat that doesn't require a PhD to operate,
17. install blinds and keep them closed at night,
18. caulk everything,
19. ceiling fans,
20. daylighting via skylights, light shelves (a system of mirrors that bounces light deeper into homes), wall cuts, clerestory windows, light tubes (lenses that channel sunlight via tubes coated with highly reflective materials into living spaces) and light bottles (soda pop bottles partially filled with water (which also contain bleach to keep out bacteria and alcohol to prevent freezing) placed in roof structures to bring light into interior spaces).

If you want to be still more green, trade in your old car for a smaller hybrid, take public transit, car share, live closer to where you work or, better yet, work from home.

Adding In-Home Apartments or Granny Flats

One of the things you can do that will add a great deal of value to your principal residence or your residential rental portfolio is add in-home apartments, granny flats in backyards or sideyards and above-garage apartments.

If it's your principal residence, this has the useful advantage that you don't have to travel very far to keep an eye on the place. Also, a portion of your realty taxes and other costs become tax deductible along with your mortgage (or, in places like Canada, interest on that part of your mortgage which funded the new apartment become tax deductible) since you are earning income from a portion of your home.

I lived for a while with my girlfriend in Santa Cruz, California while she attended UCSC. We stayed in a granny flat built in the backyard of 1011 Oceanside Avenue*; its address was 1011 and ½ Oceanside. It was a tiny one-bedroom, sunlit place with a wonderful garden. It had a galley kitchen, a long living/dining area and a bathroom that opened both to the bedroom and the main living space.

(* Address has been changed.)

I got to know the lady living in the main house (which we called the Big House); she seemed incredibly old but was probably no older than I am now (61). I asked her why she built the granny flat.

"I did it because I needed the extra income but also, umm, because I like young people and students."

It turned out that her children and grandchildren had practically forgotten about her—she was almost always alone. She built the place for financial reasons certainly but also for company and security. She felt better with us living in her backyard.

Years later when I revisited the place with my oldest son, Andrew, I was shocked to find that the center of Santa Cruz was still a mess from an earthquake two decades earlier but even more surprised to find that the young couple staying in that granny flat with their baby had the same last name as me. Talk about synchronicity.

That experience stayed with me and later we built a version of that flat; floor plans are show below.

The functional program is—

1. high ranch style bungalow with attached single car garage;
2. ground floor, ½ level up, 2-bedroom, 1-bath unit;
3. lower level, ½ level down, 2-bedroom, 1-bath apartment with separate side entrance;
4. single utility space with shared washer/dryer.

What makes this design interesting is the fact that with the addition of one door or its removal, you have either two, 2-bedroom, upper and lower apartments or one single family, 4-bedroom, 2-bath home. So over time, its use can change from, say, a single family home to a residential 2-unit rental property or perhaps you might use the lower level for a home office (it has its own entrance) while you live upstairs (or vice versa) or maybe you have an adult child moving back home with their own infant and they can now live independently downstairs while you live upstairs.

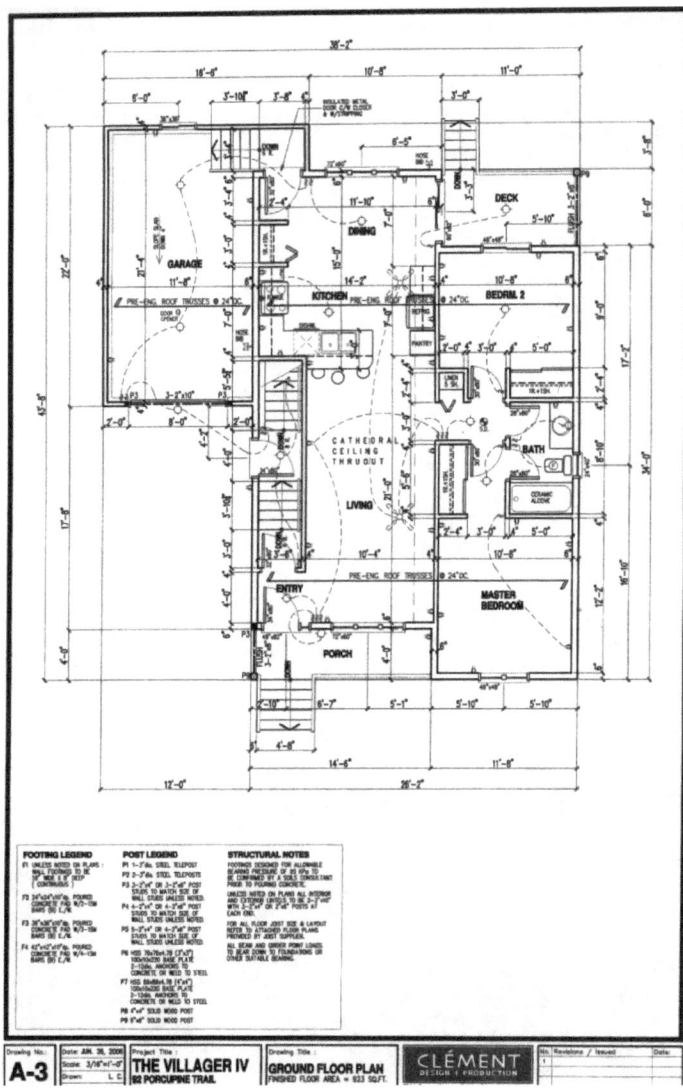

Later on, we developed alternative models including a version which was a two story home with a similar lower level unit. Again, take out one door, and it became a single family, 5-bedroom, 3 and ½ bath home. Re-hang that door and it changed into a 3-bedroom, 2 and ½ bath, 2-story home with a 2-bedroom, 1-bath, in-home apartment on the lower level with its own side entrance.

By bringing the home out of the ground by a ½ level, the lower level became less of a basement; it was more light-filled and more easily accessible being only a few steps below grade.

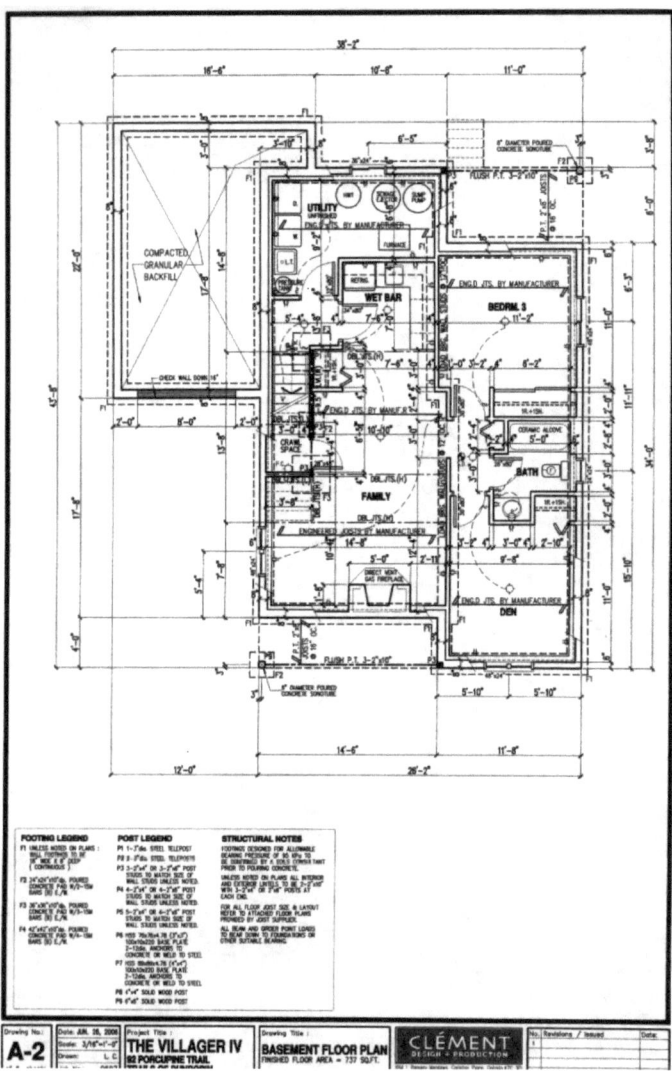

Here are the floor plans of that 2-story model—

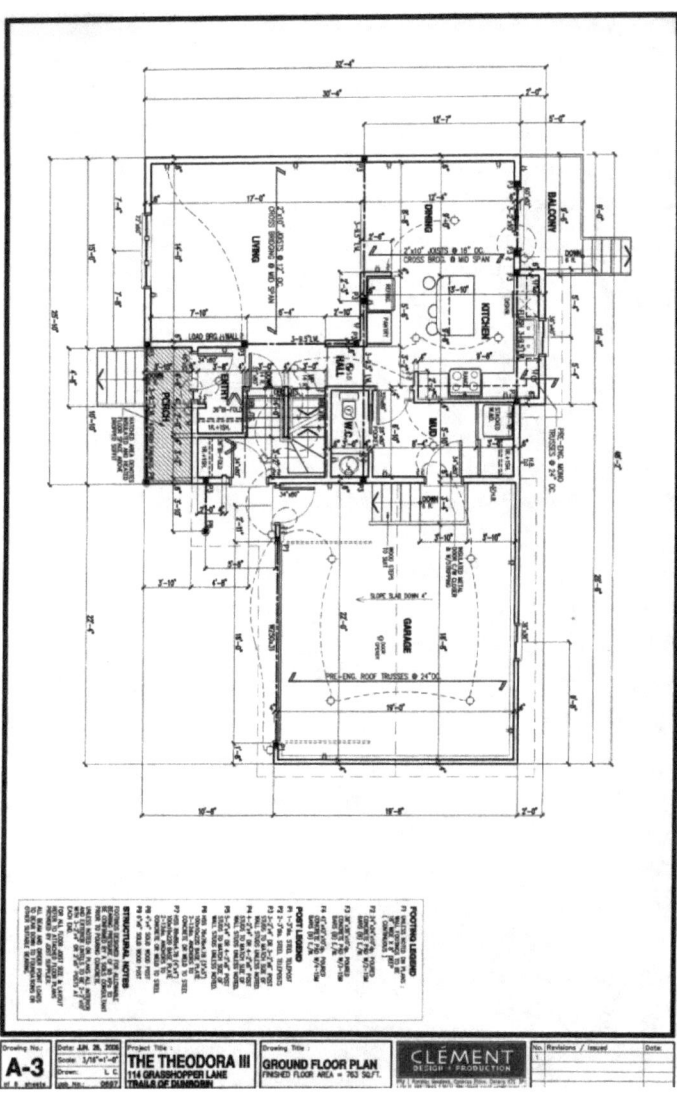

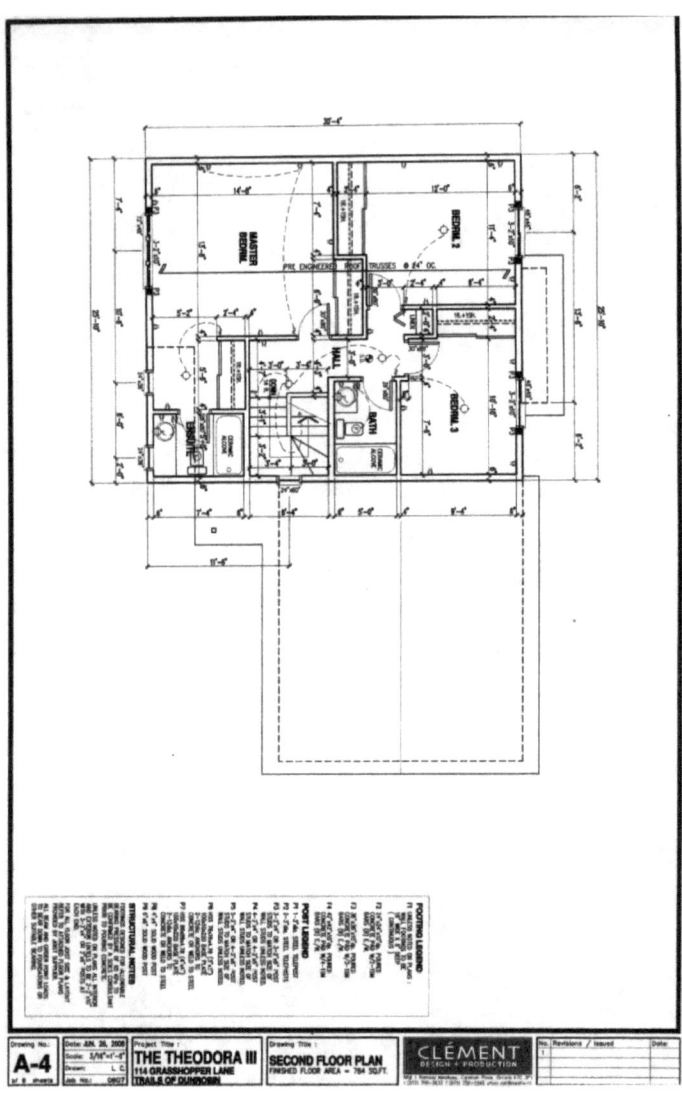

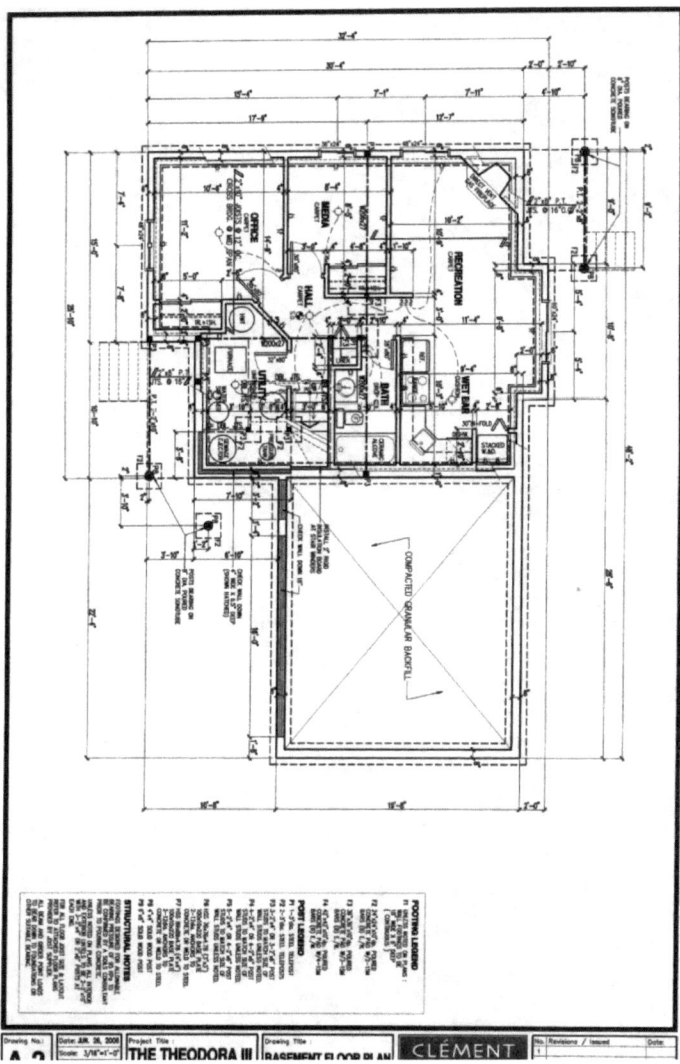

Here's a case study based on the experience of a client of mine—she's a single mother who has recently bought an investment property. Frankly, the property was a mess but she was able to buy it at a good price taking into account the work that needed to be done to bring it up to spec and it was in a good location with excellent rental prospects. The area is also experiencing strong asset growth. Again, place and street names have been changed to protect her privacy.

123 Ivanhoe Avenue, Anycity, USA

Purchase Price	$225,000				
Legals	$900.00	0.40%			
Transfer Taxes	$2,250	1%			
Total	$228,150				
Foundation repair	$20,000				
Tree removal	$4,500				
Interior renos	$55,000				
Sub-total	$79,500				
Contingencies	$6,360	8%			
Total	$85,860				
Total cost	$314,010				
Mortgage	$235,507.50	75%	3%	25	YRS
Equity	$78,502.50				
Rent					
Upper	$1,475				
Lower	$1,175				
	$2,650				
	$31,800	per yr			
Vacancy	($1,908)	6%			
Net	$29,892				
Property taxes	($2,198.07)	0.7%			
Insurance	($1,099.04)	0.35%			
Misc	($2,512.08)	0.80%			
Net net	$24,083	per yr			
Mortgage	($13,524.69)				
NOI	$10,558				
ROE	13.4%	p.a.			
House inflation	3.5%	p.a.			
irr					
0	($78,502.50)				
1	$10,558				
2	$10,558				
3	$124,886.90				
irr	25.4%	p.a.			
Sale price	$348,148.50				
Commission	($17,407.42)	5%			
Legals	($870.37)	0.25%			
Net	$329,870.70				

	Principal paid
1	($6,459.47)
2	($6,653.25)
3	($6,852.85)
	($19,965.57)
Mortgage due	$215,541.93

(Please note that all spreadsheet numbers in this document are approximate only. Errors and omissions excepted.)

This project is an incredibly important part of her retirement plan; her goal is to buy two more such units, pay off the mortgages on all three rental properties as well as her principal residence and live on the proceeds. She started late (she's 51 at the time of writing) but she is about halfway to her goal.

She is expecting income from her (present and future) rental properties of about $80,000 annually by the time she is 71. She will have inflation protection in two forms—first, she will increase rents at or above the inflation rate and second, capital appreciation of real property has tended to exceed consumer price inflation in her city for many decades. This is her only hope since she has no independent pension plan and government-funded plans cannot possibly hope to keep up with the growth of the elder community. She's on her own in every way.

The fastest growing demographic in the U.S. and Canada is the 100 ups so people (especially women who tend to outlive men by at least 8 years) have to plan for much longer time horizons than a world where average life expectancies were much shorter not that long ago.

Just to put things in perspective, you would need to save $11,428,571.43 to generate $80,000 a year in income at 0.7% p.a. from your bank's "Power Savings Account". Even if you could somehow double that boosting returns to 1.4%, you would still need more than $5.7 million in cash to generate what she can do with three rental properties. If she needs to, she will further increase her retirement income by renting out rooms in her 3-bedroom principal residence. In other words, she will cope.

Just in case you feel badly because your investment returns are so low, comfort yourself by reflecting on the fact that both Google and Apple (which have billions of dollars of cash on their respective balance sheets) also have to content themselves with 0.7% p.a. returns on their vast cash hoards. There are a lot of smart people who work at those companies.

For people worried about their jobs or tired of disappointing returns on their mutual funds, 401 (k) plans, t-bills, savings accounts, checking accounts, insurance policies, independent pension plans, stock portfolios and friends with can't-miss business ideas, you could do worse than follow this lady's model.

In some jurisdictions, you may be able to borrow from your other investments to generate the equity you need to fund a real estate portfolio. This can boost your returns on your investments and create further tax advantages since interest paid on money invested in for-profit ventures can be tax deductible from income and such interest flowing back to registered retirement accounts may be tax deferred.

(Please note that every investment strategy including a real estate one should be vetted by your attorney and tax accountant. Nothing in this document provides any tax or legal advice. Scenarios are for illustration purposes only.)

Real Estate Investing Made Easy

Buy Some Commercial Property

Most small scale real estate investors think they can't buy commercial. "We don't understand commercial," they'll say. "It's too big for us." "That's just for Banks, Pen Funds, REITs, Publicly Traded behemoths and Insurance companies."

Nothing could be further from the truth. There is a lot of commercial real estate dominated by the little guy including:

a) mini storage,
b) small retail plazas,
c) office and industrial condos,
d) travel apartments,
e) land development.

Over the last three decades, we've built and owned all of these!
Here's a 10,000 square foot plaza we built in a suburban location:

Village Plaza

We also developed Blue Heron storage in another suburb, inner city Presidential Executive Travel Apartments (PETA), office and industrial condos in industrial parks and we did numerous land development projects including Robertson Mews (which had single family homes, townhomes, 1 and 2-bedroom condos as well as a retirement residence) and Briarbrook, an 850-home subdivsion with a shopping mall, gas station and other commercial facilities.

Here is a photo of one of the storage buildings we built, owned and managed under the Blue Heron banner:

Real Estate Investing Made Easy

Storage Building (Front Units for RVs/Boats)
(note the skylights on the front roof)

People are right about one thing—you do have to stay out of the way of the big guys because they can kill you. The COC (Cost of Capital) for a Pension Fund or Insurance Co today is less than 1.5% while for most small investors in commercial it is anywhere from 4% to as much as 12% or even 15% p.a. If you give your competitors that kind of advantage, they'll demolish you. So small investors cannot invest in mega shopping malls or major office buildings even if they have the equity to do it.

But don't tell me you can't buy a $229,000 industrial condo to diversify your real estate portfolio, you certainly can.

Here's a 3-D rendering of an industrial condo that one of my sons (Matthew Firestone) is developing for owner occupancy.

What you'll find in commercial is:

Bruce M Firestone 29

a) There is no rent control (parties to commercial transactions, both leases and sales, are both supposed to be sophisticated and equal in terms of information and access to resources) so if a tenant acts up, commercial landlords can distrain them which means simply posting a notice in many jurisdictions or delivering a letter for, say, non-payment of rent or some other significant breach of contract and they're gone in no time and you can re-rent the place.

b) Commercial landlords typically want three to five year leases (or longer, ten years is quite common for retail leasing and 25 years is not unknown in Europe) so they don't have to re-rent and fix up the place every year like residential landlords do.

c) Again, commercial landlords have to make sure they have a good team around them—a deal making lawyer (as opposed to a deal killing one), an accountant who can do more than count (i.e., s/he can help you structure your affairs to be tax efficient and creditor proof), a realtor who actually knows commercial and a mortgage broker (this is just as essential in residential real estate as well). You can do your own property management here if you care to since it tends to be far less intensive than the residential kind.

d) Capitalization rates in commercial tend to be better because there tends to be less competition from know-nothing, overly eager buyers of residential property who tend to buy high/sell low.

MINI STORAGE

In addition to building, owning and managing some mini storage units for our own account, I am or have been an adviser to a few including Cosmic Storage, Public Storage, CP Mini Storage and others. Recently, one of them was going to construct a car/boat/RV storage barn on his site. I looked at the economics with him which were not bad but not great either.

Basically, he was going to build an unheated garage 50 feet by 80 feet which could hold at capacity 20 vehicles of assorted sizes—cars/boats/RVs. The building had one large door (12 feet wide by 14 feet high) at each end. Ceiling height was a clear 18 feet. The vehicles were to be packed in like sardines leaving just enough room for a skinny driver to exit the last column of vehicles. Once they are parked, they are there for the season (six months from November to April).

People pay depending on size—cars are $55 per month, boats are $65 and RVs $85. They have to buy and stay for the season.

Off season revenues are less—far fewer people park indoors in northern areas during the summer. There are a few who do it—to keep the sun off expensive cars for example. So let's assume, he gets 55% of his winter season revenues during the summer. (This is being generous.)

His cost to construct including hard, soft, financing, building permit costs as well as development charges for his 4,000 square foot building was $185,500 or $46.38 per square foot. I have also included the value of the land in this figure. His revenues for the year less operating costs and property taxes are $9,672. This is his NOI, Net Operating Income.

Cap rates (aka capitalization rates) are calculated by dividing NOI by SP, Selling Price. Let's assume his SP is his cost to construct plus the value of his land which is $185,500.

Thus, his Cap Rate = $9,672/$185,500 or 5.2%.

Cap rates are notional, rules of thumb widely used in the real estate industry basically because they are easy to calculate. But they do not take into account anything other than cash on cash returns missing out on forced savings and the wealth effect. Which as we saw above can add substantially to overall returns.

So to really calculate his ROI, Return on Investment, we have to use the IRR, Internal rate of Return.

In this case, his IRR turns out to be 9.6% p.a. It's higher than his cap rate which is what you would expect once you factor in that over the first five years of a 25 year mortgage, his tenants have paid off ($17,078.62) of his principal for him. (All my calculations are shown below in ADDENDUM 1. You can also download my spreadsheets in .xls format from our server so you can fool around with them on your own. The links are also included below.) In addition, I have assumed that the value of his property increases by 2% p.a. which is conservative for his area where property values have tended to increase fairly secularly over many decades at anywhere from 2.5% to 3.5% p.a. in almost all sectors.

Much of the difference in ROI when we compare his cap rate (5.2%) with his IRR (9.6%) comes from the increase in value of his property. Remember my advice above—I am not comfortable relying on ever increasing selling prices to bail you out of a poor cash-on-cash return.

So whether you rely on cap rates or go to the extra trouble of calculating IRRs (which you should do), I would not advise you to proceed with this project as proposed. The returns are too skinny—you can test the sensitivity of the results to say changes in construction costs or increases in vacancy rates. That's easy to do since all the cells in my spreadsheets are linked. I change one thing and, presto, excel spits out a whole new set of answers.

So let's see what happens when we change one variable at a time. Let's suppose that hard construction costs jump from $25 to $35 per sq ft. Now you are *losing* more than $2,000 per year operating this vehicle storage barn which means you are *paying* people so they can park their fancy cars/boats and RVs in your building. This is BAD.

Your cap rate has fallen below your cost of capital (ugh)—it's now 4.2% while you are paying 4.5% on your mortgage. Your IRR is just 6.1% which is horrible for a private investor. Still you are being rescued by the fact that you can presumably sell the place after five years to another person (sucker) at a price higher than you paid to build it in the first place and you have paid off some of your mortgage too.

I tried one more case—Case 3 where vacancy rates in the summer season went to 70% (up from 45%). His cap rate drops to 4.4% and his IRR moves down to 6.7%. All of these cases can be downloaded from our server using the links provided in ADDENDUM 1.

OK, so this project is a big NO GO, right? Wrong. Let's try it again but this time, let's add some differentiated value (pixie dust).

We are still going to use the barn for its intended purpose during the winter season—storing vehicles. But in the spring, let's kick everyone out.

Why? Well, I remembered something that happened years ago when my wife and I were visiting Stratford, Ontario to see a few plays. One Saturday morning, late in the fall season, we drove around the countryside. About an hour northeast of Stratford and about the same driving time northwest of Toronto, we came over a low ridge and, at the confluence of two undistinguished two-lane highways, we saw several thousand cars parked in what looked like a farmer's field.

We stopped. What would bring 1,000s of folks to a field at 0830 on a Saturday? Turns out it was a Mennonite market garden selling fresh produce (fruits and vegetables), canned goods, honey, maple syrup and a myriad of other products including Mennonite furniture, wagons and handicrafts. There were also many non-Mennonite stalls although many of these appeared to be selling nothing more than trash and trinkets.

Being a garrulous type of person, I stopped people and asked why they came and how often—the answers clearly pointed to a strong desire to: a) buy local, b) know where their food was coming from, c) buy organic, d) support the Mennonites, e) satisfy a quest for adventure. Now this occurred in the 1990s long before it became fashionable to do anything like this.

I've been carrying the idea around with me ever since and I suggested it to my friends at Cosmic Storage—set up a flea market in their barn building each summer. This is the kind of thing that suits the owner of a place with a name like "Cosmic" Storage—he has a marketing program that says each storage customer receives (FREE) an organic garden plot the exact same size as any unit they rent. If you rent a 10' × 20' unit, you qualify for a garden plot of the same size.

If you look at my friend's logo, you'll get an idea about the place:

Being Cosmic

So I suggested he turn the place into a 'Whole Earth' farmers' market every summer. But what does that do to the economics of the new build? A whole lot, it turns out.

He'll have room for about 26, 10' × 10' stalls in his 4,000 square foot barn. His season is May to October which means 26 weekends. The place will be open Saturday and Sunday during the shoulder seasons and probably Thursday to Sunday in high season. I assumed that they would get $185 per stall per weekend (or week) and have a vacancy rate of 30%. What does this to his NOI, Cap Rate and IRR? Magic!

His NOI jumps from $9,672 per annum to $74,861. His Cap Rate goes from 5.2% to 40.4% and his IRR from 9.6% p.a. to a whopping 142.1% p.a. Wow.

Now that's a REAL business.

Also, the number of years it takes to recover the cost of the new build (including its land cost) drops from an ugly 19.2 years to just 2.5.

TRAVEL APARTMENTS

I've always liked the Executive Travel Apartment business. We ran PETA for many years. We owned 16 units. We rented them out by making HR personnel at (mostly) local tech companies aware that they were available. They would bring in new hires (often with family in tow) for assignments ranging in duration from 1, 2 or 3 months to indefinite and rather than putting them up at local hotels at a cost of $300+ per day, they would rent from PETA which had 1, 2 and 3-bedroom fully furnished suites ready-to-go at $100 per day.

Later on, we used them for NHL players who were traded to the local team. It's a lot nicer to live in a travel apartment for a few months than a hotel room.

The units all had lock boxes (which could be reprogrammed after a guest left) on them so people could arrive at all hours of the day or night and just let themselves in. We provided weekly maid service (at an extra charge). By adding furniture and the basics (like soap!) plus having cable TV and phone service on (today, you would obviously add Internet, wi-fi and Netflix), we bumped the rents for the units from $1,200 per month to $3,000 per month. Today, they would fetch $4,500 per month.

Damage to the units was low, collections were a breeze and it was a mostly fun business to be in.

And, oh by the way, PETA was not subject to the rent control.

The only downside that we experienced was that vacancies tended to be higher (in the range of 6 to 8%) than typical residential rentals (1 to 3%). When you are renting for short periods like one to three months instead of a more typical one year term, you are bound to get higher vacancies if only because as one person or family leaves say mid-month, the next group may not come in until the beginning of the following month.

(A former student of mine got into this business a few years ago and she discovered a new way to finance her investment that I thought was very clever. You can read about her in the ADDENDUM at the end of this document.)

Buy Some Land

My two boys own some land near our home that they use as a parking lot. It doesn't make much money. It's just a place holder—an interim use.

Land forms part of your holdings because they aren't making any more of it. This is the one area where it may be OK to lose money every month.

Here's an example. Clients of mine bought a residential building lot in rural part of the city three and a half years ago for $70k. They put 50% down and got a bank loan for the balance. So every month, they HAD to pay their bank, right? (Banks have a nasty habit of insisting on this actually.)

So every month, they are paying off some of their mortgage—remember this is a form of forced savings.

Bill and Cathy (not their real names) paid off about 2/3 of their mortgage over the three year period they owned the lot. Where did that money go? To their bank? Not really, it went into the land.

Thank goodness it didn't go into their savings account because we know what would have happened to it if it did—they would have spent it on stuff. Nope, it's in the land.

We sold their lot for $135k which means after paying realtor and legal fees when it completed, they'll have around $127k less the $12k they still owe on their mortgage which means they'll have about $115k in cash on hand from their original $35k investment made three years ago. Not too shabby.

There's just no way they could have saved $115,000 in three years.

I'll tell you another story. A friend of mine, an elder now in his late 80s wanted to start a pharma distribution business back in the day. But like most (all) entrepreneurs, he had NO money. So he went to the 'real estate store' (that's what he calls it). He went to a number of brokerages and befriended some agents. He asked them to show him their *worst* properties, the most neglected, the boggiest, wettest pieces of garbage land they had in their inventory (i.e., listed for sale). Not, you must agree, he is not a typical realtor client?

Over the next few years, he bought more than 3,000 acres of land in and around his hometown (for as little as $150 per acre) getting as much as 90% STB (Seller Take Back) mortgages from owners (who were so keen to dump these unwanted properties that they would do almost anything to speed up the process). Thus, he only had to come up with 10% downpayments most of which he borrowed from his brother, a well-to-do veterinarian and a war hero to boot.

Three years later, at age 32, he went into his bank and got himself a $500,000 LOC (Line of Credit).

"Have any collateral?" they asked him.

"Sure," he said. "Lots! I'm a big shooter! I'm a ginormous landowner!"

He even told them he had an interim use—he'd leased out some of his lands to farmers and ranchers (true) and even owned some cattle and sheep himself.

Now the latter wasn't entirely true* so when the bank manager asked to see some of his land *and* some of his herd, he was stumped but only for a minute or two. He subsequently trucked in a bunch of cattle and sheep (borrowed them). You have to laugh—ranchers traditionally don't pasture sheep and cattle together but the city slicker bank manager didn't know that. He was impressed by the young man, his herd and his extensive landholdings so he approved the loan.

(* Please don't do this. It's OK to tell the smart truth but never a lie).

His pharma distribution business did exceptionally well and he sold it decades later and retired to the life of a country gentleman.

Now there is an epilogue to this story that is worth telling. Whatever happened to those useless 3,000 acres? The city expanded and they became worth millions more, some of which I subsequently sold for him.

Conclusion

Real estate has some attributes that are unique to this asset class. Here are ten of them:

1. You can rent real estate to third parties. (Try that with gold or stocks assuming you are not using exotic financial instruments.)

2. By renting to a third party you are benefiting from a wealth effect; every year a renter is paying off part of your mortgage for you—when you sell that property, the decrease in principal owing goes into your pocket (assuming that the price you sell for is more than what you paid for the property plus transaction costs).

3. You receive unearned (and untaxed) rent on self-occupied property after your mortgage is retired.

4. When your city builds infrastructure around you, when your neighbors improve their properties, when the density and overall area of the city increases, demand for your property increases without you having done a thing—as a result your property value benefits from positive externalities.

5. In many countries, you are allowed to deduct a non-cash capital cost allowance against income—a significant tax advantage from holding real estate assets.

6. Real estate generally doesn't go out of fashion.

7. Land, unlike, say, ideas, is in fixed supply with many cities further restricting supply by limiting urban expansion which is great if you are a sitting owner. Not so great if you are a first time homebuyer or newly minted real estate entrepreneur.

8. The amount of real estate consumed per capita has been steadily increasing almost everywhere for a long time and average household size has been shrinking so even where populations are stable, increasing slowly or even falling somewhat, demand for space is increasing.

9. In-migration to urban areas from rural areas is continuing everywhere as cities benefit from network effects so overall demand for urban real estate tends to increase secularly.

10. Lastly, real estate offers you a unique opportunity to develop a sustainable business model even if you aren't a genius. Real estate develops a 'concession' or 'franchise' for its owners because once you own a particular location, axiomatically, no one else can own at that location.

Everyone knows that real estate is all about LOCATION, LOCATION, LOCATION but perhaps people don't realize why it is so crucial. For you to have a business that will nurture you and your family for a long period of time, you need to have some type of sustainable competitive advantage.

Imagine how difficult it is to run a company like Apple or how difficult it is to paint like Rembrandt. Not everyone can be a Steve Jobs or create artwork like Rembrandt Harmenszoon van Rijn. Real estate held in fee simple (the highest form of title an owner can have) gives you a franchise forever that tough competitors like Microsoft or Apple or Google can't take away from you—IT'S A BUSINESS MODEL FOR DUMMIES.

A friend of mine owns a great site at the corner of two major avenues in a fast growing city. He comes from a tech background but his chosen personal investment vehicle is real estate. He and his partner built a new, high concept strip mall (not intended as an oxymoron) on top of the old foundation of a previous building and, because of its high traffic location, great visibility and design features, they got rents that are about 1/3 higher than other nearby properties. I mean how difficult can it be to own a great location and have people come up to you, one after the other, to offer you top dollar for your space, year after year?

Let me end this by saying that there is no easy business and real estate investing is not a hobby nor is it a source of the holy grail—passive income. In my view, there is no holy grail. If you want passive income with little or no work, put your money in treasury bills and collect 0.7% interest on them which is horrible.

No, sorry, if you own real estate, you'll have to work hard at it—buy smart, assemble a trusted team, become expert at managing your assets, sell when it is wise to do so, understand finance, construction, renovation, design and much more… So this booklet is dedicated to people who are diligent, work hard, learn what there is to learn and are prepared to do what's needed to become successful. Remember, the harder you work, the luckier you'll get.

@ProfBruce

[Prof Bruce is available for real estate coaching sessions. For more information, please contact Ms Nina Brooks, ninabrooks@rogers.com.]

ADDENDUM 1
Spreadsheets for Calculating Cap Rates and IRRs for Vehicle Storage Buildings

You can see the numbers I used for the base case below but you can also download it and the spreadsheets for the other variations of the base case from our server (in .xls format) using these links:
http://www.eqjournal.org/mini-storage-revisited-base-case.xls
http://www.eqjournal.org/mini-storage-revisited-case-2-higher-construction-costs.xls
http://www.eqjournal.org/mini-storage-revisited-case-3-higher-vacancy-rate.xls
http://www.eqjournal.org/mini-storage-revisited-differentiated-value.xls

Car/Boat/RV Storage Revisited
Base Case
    Building 50 ft 80 ft 4000 sq ft
Vehicle Storage 200 sq ft/vehicle
Number Vehicles 20
RVs $85 per mth 5 $425
Boats $65 per mth 5 $325
Cars $55 per mth 10 $550
Revenues $1,300 per mth
Season November to April 6 mths
Revenues $7,800 per season
Off Season Revenues May to October 55% $4,290
Total Revenues $12,090 per yr
Operating Costs & Property Taxes 20% ($2,418)
NOI (Net Operating Income) $9,672 per yr
    Cost to Build (Unheated)
    Construction $25 per sq ft $100,000
Soft Costs 11% $11,000
Financing 10% $2,500 3 mths
Bldg Permit $10.50 per sq ft $42,000.00
Land $30,000.00
Total Cost $185,500 $46.38 19.2 yrs to recover building cost
    Cap Rate (NOI/SP) 5.2% p.a.
    IRR 25% equity
    0 ($46,375)
1 $289.55
2 $289.55
3 $289.55
4 $289.55
5 $71,785.77
    IRR 9.6% p.a.
    SP (Selling Price) 2.00% increase in value each year
SP (Selling Price) $204,806.99 Year 5
Less REALTOR and Legal Fees ($11,264.38) 5.50%
Net SP $193,542.60
    Mortgage $139,125.00 4.5% 25 yrs
Mortgage ($9,382.45) per yr
    Principal $139,125.00
Principal Repaid
1 ($3,121.83)
2 ($3,262.31)

3 ($3,409.12)
4 ($3,562.53)
5 ($3,722.84)
Total Principal Repaid ($17,078.62)
Mortgage Balance $122,046.38

ADDENDUM 2
Executive Travel Apartments—Reducing your Capital Requirements

A student recently introduced me a new form of Bootstrap Capital, or at least, one I hadn't considered before. It seems obvious to me now but I think it takes some creativity to apply it to any business model.

She is in the Executive Travel Apartment (ETA) business—those are extended stay suites that executives use and many prefer to a long stay in a hotel room.

It is a very capital intensive business: she needs equity to buy her units, renovate them and furnish them. She can reduce her capital needs by mortgaging the units using high LTV (Loan to Value) ratios and leasing (or leasing to own) the furniture she needs for each unit. Still her equity requirements are non-trivial.

She came up with a very inventive method of expanding her budding empire without having to bring in a partner or sell her soul to finance companies.

A form of bootstrapping is to lower the level of capital you require in the first place.

She can charge about $3,500 to $4,500 per month for her ETAs, about $120 to $150 per night for a one, two or three bedroom unit which is fully furnished, the Internet and TV work, the VOiP phones are on and there is a starter kit (soap, salt and pepper, bread, milk, etc.) on hand. Just let yourself in using the lockbox combination, and relax, you're home.

Because these are ETAs, she comes under the Innkeepers Act and not the RTA (Residential Tenancy Act) so she is much less likely to have trouble with her tenants than a typical residential tenancy where delinquency is high, collections are tough and getting rid of them (evicting them) is even tougher.

A typical unit can cost her $200,000 or more to buy (with anywhere from 5% to 25% equity required), $20,000 to renovate and another $10k or so to furnish. So each unit can easily consume $70 or $80k of equity. Other ETA operators solve this problem by selling the units to investors and keeping management in their hands plus a share of ownership.

She came up with another way—what if she went to residential landlords and told them: "I will lease some (or all) of your units for repackaging as ETAs." From a Landlord's POV, that takes him or her out of the purview of the RTA and he or she now only has to manage one tenant (the ETA operator). The ETA operator worries about furnishing the units, renting them out, managing and maintaining them, etc.

In the buy scenario described above, she will need $80,000 in equity per door. If she rents each unit out for $4,000 per month and has a mortgage at 6% with a 20 year amortization period, she will be left with a NOI (Net Operating Income) after deducting a vacancy allowance, marketing costs, admin and contingencies of about $1,077 per unit per month.

If she sublets units from a cooperative Landlord at $1,400 monthly, she is left with less—just $766.49 per month per unit. This is because she is paying less on her mortgage than she is in rent to the Landlord.

But in the first case, she needs $80k of equity; in the second case, she only needs $30k.

Now her simple ROE (Return on Equity) is 16.2% p.a. when she buys her own units versus a whopping 30.7% when she rents them instead. (See the spreadsheet below.)

Now this model ignores the wealth effect of owning your own units (the annual paydown of your mortgage principal, in effect, by your tenants) and real estate inflation (that goes solely to the equity holder).

If I took those factors into account, the ROEs would probably be a lot closer*. But that doesn't matter if she can't afford to expand her business because the equity demands of the first model are too high for her to handle.

So the obvious choice is to do both—own some units and sublet some. As her cashflow improves, she should probably be buying relatively more of her units.

But at least initially, from her POV, her capital requirements have dropped from the $70 to $80k per door range to $10 to $30k per door and her ability to grow the business faster has just taken a quantum leap upwards.

Another client recently showed me how he could acquire inventory for his retail store at a negative cost to him—other retailers are paying him to feature their products and services in his outlet store. They pay him a monthly fee for this plus they give him a percentage of each of their products or services that he sells for them on consignment.

We are now busy applying this philosophy to other types of businesses with great effect.

* If we take into account the wealth effect and the impact of real estate inflation, the two rates of return (this time measured using the IRR instead of the simple ROE ratio) are, in fact, closer. In the 'buy' scenario, the return increases from 16.2% p.a. to 22.8% while for the 'sub let' scenario, the return remains that same at 30.7%.

The latter doesn't change because, in this model, I have assumed that when she sells the business at the end of year 7 (an arbitrary time line, I might add), she realizes exactly what she put in initially for renovations and furnishings. Of course, in reality what she gets for the business would depend on what she and a Buyer agree to which could be greater or less than this amount. Nevertheless, in order not to bias the comparative analysis, it seemed reasonable to make this assumption.

You can examine the spreadsheet below or download it in .xls format from my server at: http://www.ottawarealestatenews.ca/ETAs.xls.

ETAs
Buy the Units
Cost per Unit $200,000
Equity ($50,000) 25%
Mortgage $150,000 75%
Interest 6% p.a.
Amortization 20 years
Monthly Payment ($1,089.81) to Lender
Renovations ($20,000)
Furniture ($10,000)
($30,000)
Interest 10% p.a.
Amortization 7 years
Monthly Payment ($513.51)
Total Cost ($1,603.32)
Monthly Rent $4,000
Marketing ($320) 8%
Vacancy ($480) 12%
Other ($240) 6%
Contingencies ($280) 7%
NOI $1,077 per month
Equity ($80,000)
ROE 16.2% per annum
Year
0 ($80,000.00)
1 $ 12,920.15
2 $ 12,920.15
3 $ 12,920.15
4 $ 12,920.15
5 $ 12,920.15
6 $ 12,920.15
7 $ 167,186.31 $ 12,920.15 $ 124,266.15 $30,000

IRR 22.8% p.a. Assumes the business is sold
and the sale price of the biz
R.E. Inflation 2.75% equals the investment in
Selling Price $ 241,825.90 furniture and renovations.
Agency Fees ($12,091.29) 5%
Legal Fees/Closing Costs ($1,105.00)
Net $ 228,629.60
Principal Repaid
1 ($5,436.91)
2 ($5,763.13)
3 ($6,108.91)
4 ($6,475.45)
5 ($6,863.98)
6 ($7,275.81)
7 ($7,712.36)
Total Principal Repaid ($45,636.55)
Mortgage Balance Due $104,363.45
Net to Seller $ 124,266.15 on completion
 SubLet the Units
 Cost per Unit 0
Equity 0
Mortgage 0
Monthly Payment ($1,400) to Landlord
Renovations ($20,000)
Furniture ($10,000)
($30,000)
Interest 10% p.a.
Amortization 7 years
Monthly Payment ($513.51)
Total Cost ($1,913.51)
Monthly Rent $4,000
Marketing ($320) 8%
Vacancy ($480) 12%
Other ($240) 6%
Contingencies ($280) 7%
NOI $766.49 per month
Equity ($30,000)
ROE 30.7% per annum
Year
0 ($30,000)
1 $9,197.84
2 $9,197.84
3 $9,197.84
4 $9,197.84
5 $9,197.84
6 $9,197.84
7 $39,197.84 $9,197.84 $30,000
IRR 30.7% per annum Assumes the business is sold
and the sale price of the biz
equals the investment in furniture and renovations.
E&OE

About the Author

Bruce M Firestone
B Eng (Civil), M Eng-Sci, PhD

Bruce applied to go to McGill University in Montreal at age 14, arrived after turning 15, and graduated as a civil engineer before legally becoming an adult (then, age 21). He was rejected in his first job search because he was considered a "child," not legally responsible for his actions. Three and a half weeks later, he was living in Sydney, Australia. A new and exciting labour government had just been elected. The first two things Prime Minister Gough Whitlam did were to recall Aussie troops from Vietnam and to lower the age of majority to 18.

Bruce worked for the New South Wales government, doing operations research and building mixed integer programming models while continuing his education at the University of New South Wales, where he obtained his Masters of Engineering-Science degree, and then at the Australian National University in Canberra, where he received his PhD in urban economics.

He was among the first group in Australia to fly hang-gliders and not die. He has traveled to and worked in the United States, Sri Lanka, New Zealand, India, Canada, Australia and many other nations. He has been, at different times, an engineer, a real estate developer, a hockey executive (founder of NHL team the Ottawa Senators, Canadian Tire Centre and the Senators Foundation—a children's charity), a university professor, a keynote speaker, a consultant, coach, mentor, art collector and benefactor, writer, columnist, futurist, and novelist as well as Executive Director of not-for-profit Exploriem.org—an organization dedicated to assisting entrepreneurs, artpreneurs, and intrapreneurs everywhere. Bruce went back to school in his 50s, completed eight real estate courses and is now a real estate broker with Century 21 Explorer Realty Inc.

Bruce has taught and studied at McGill University, Laval University, the University of New South Wales, the Australian National University, Harvard University, the University of Western Ontario, Carleton University, and the University of Ottawa in subject areas that include entrepreneurship, business models, architecture, engineering, finance, urban planning, urban design, traffic and transportation planning, and development economics.

He has launched, or helped launch, more than 300 startups. Currently, he writes for three blogs—EQJournal.org (about entrepreneurship), DramatisPersonae.org (about artpreneurship and urban issues) and profbruce.tumblr.com (about life)—and moderates lively @ProfBruce and @Quantum_Entity communities on Twitter. He is also author of *Quantum Entity Trilogy*, *Real Estate Investing Made Easy*, *How to get Rich for Real*, *How to Retire Rich at Any Age, For Real*, and *Entrepreneurs Handbook II*. His upcoming novels include *Urban Nirvana and the Peradventures of Maddy Henderson*, and *Saragasso City*.

He is married to a most wonderful girl, Dawn MacMillan. They have five great kids and one fine grandson.

...

"Entrepreneurs follow a moral path when they—first, take care of their business so that, second, the business can take care of their families so that, third, their families can take care of them so that, fourth, they don't become a burden on society or their fellow human beings so that, fifth, they can help others so that, sixth, others can help their business," Prof Bruce, 2014.

His current motto is: "*Making the impossible, possible*".

...

Blogs: eqjournal.org, dramatispersonae.org and www.profbruce.tumblr.com
Twitter: @ProfBruce and @Quantum_Entity
LinkedIn: www.linkedin.com/in/profbruce
Facebook: https://www.facebook.com/QuantumEntityTrilogy
YouTube: http://www.youtube.com/user/ProfBruce and http://www.youtube.com/user/quantumentitytrilogy
Books available from: http://www.brucemfirestone.com

...

www.ingramcontent.com/pod-product-compliance
Lightning Source LLC
Chambersburg PA
CBHW040929180526
45159CB00002BA/667